With Double Blade

Jean Gill

'Jean Gill's spiky humour makes you feel as if she's caught you on barbed wire and yet makes you smile about it' – Mike Sharpe, Haverfordwest Journalist

'...cuts clean through the icing with a cynic's knife. No scalpel delicacy here, but brutal slicing through the rich cake of life, exposing flaws as well as fruit – Jean Gill doesn't give a hoot! Often, a verse that starts with saccharine romance suddenly bursts out and kicks you in the pants.' – Derek Rees, The Guardian

'Jean Gill brings off the rare feat of looking life squarely in the eye without descending into dreary cynicism.' – H.S. Milford Haven Journalist

'...the humour frequently has the effect of pointing up the stark reality with which she writes.' – Ted Griffin, Pause Magazine

'An excellent collection – I enjoyed the sharpness and insight, the word-play... strong, fresh, vivid poems' – Robert Nisbet, author

'A delicious book full of the unexpected. Highly emotive contents.' – Writing Magazine

'Moving and varied' – Dorothy Tutin

Praise for *One Sixth of a Gill*, **Finalist in the Wishing Shelf Awards and the SpaSpa Awards for Literary Fiction**
'A superb collection... so much variation in style and all equally brilliant.' Karen Maitland, The Vanishing Witch

'A FINALIST and highly recommended... The author is particularly gifted with poetry.' The Wishing Shelf Awards

2nd Edition © 2018 Jean Gill
The 13th Sign
All rights reserved.
ISBN 9791096459087
1st edition The National Poetry Foundation 1988

Cover design by Jessica Bell

Jean Gill's publications
Novels
The Troubadours Quartet
Book 4 Song Hereafter *(The 13th Sign)* 2017
Book 3 Plaint for Provence *(The 13th Sign)* 2015
Book 2 Bladesong *(The 13th Sign)* 2015
Book 1 Song at Dawn *(The 13th Sign)* 2015

Someone to Look Up To: a dog's search for love and understanding *(The 13th Sign)* 2016

Love Heals
Book 2 More Than One Kind *(The 13th Sign)* 2016
Book 1 No Bed of Roses (*The 13th Sign)* 2016

Looking for Normal (teen fiction/fact)
Book 2 Fortune Kookie *(The 13th Sign)* 2017
Book 1 Left Out *(The 13th Sign)* 2017

Non-fiction/Memoir/Travel
How Blue is my Valley *(The 13th Sign)* 2016
A Small Cheese in Provence *(The 13th Sign)* 2016
Faithful through Hard Times *(The 13th Sign)* 2017

Short Stories and Poetry
One Sixth of a Gill *(The 13th Sign)* 2014
From Bedtime On *(The 13th Sign)* 2018
With Double Blade *(The 13th Sign)* 2018

Contents

To Secretary Sandra's Golf-Ball	*1, 44*
Watching Old People	*2, 44*
Men?	*3, 43*
Nothing Personal	*4, 45*
The Aran Jumper	*5, 45*
Spring Prayer	*6, 45*
Pandora's Box	*7, 46*
Integrity	*8, 47*
Birthday Present for My Father	*9, 47*
Never Forget Your Welsh	*10, 47*
Trivial Pursuits?	*12, 48*
Re.Generation	*13, 48*
Equality	*14, 49*
'Last Lesson' – but worse	*15, 50*
Commissioned Work for Mr Pudner	*16, 50*
Defective System	*18, 50*
Poet Dreams	*19, 51*
Tunisian Compromise	*20, 51*
For Members of F.A.	*21, 52*
Study in Grey	*22, 53*
Defined by Loss	*23, 53*
Farmers Shoot First	*24, 54*
Arthur's Plea	*25, 55*
Note from Guinevere to Lancelot	*26, 55*
Lancelot Insane	*27, 56*
A Night at the Theatre	*28, 57*
To Bluebeard	*29, 57*
After the Mexican Earthquake, 1985	*30, 58*
Merry-Go-Round	*32, 59*
Which Club Are You In?	*33, 59*
Duet	*34, 60*
The Three Wise Monkeys	*36, 60*

A Bad Day Technologically Speaking	*37, 61*
YXX?	*38, 62*
The Lady and the Minstrel	*40, 63*
Young Love	*41, 64*
Not Just Married	*42, 64*
Leave in Silence	*43, 64*

Section 2
The Stories Behind the Poems   *44*

Acknowledgements

Border decoration under Creative Commons License from www.webdesignhot.com

Cover artwork
Bee: © Larry Rains; Woman with pink hair: © Sytnik

Poems published in Outposts, Poetry Nottingham, Envoi, Pause

Special thanks to Johnathon Clifford, the National Poetry Foundation, for his mentoring, editing and personal encouragement

For my mother and for John

Introduction

I see poetry as the perfect marriage between form and content, which is why I've always written in so many different forms. The emotion comes in words, a shape, a rhythm. When I give a poetry reading, I tell the stories behind the poems and so I thought it was time to add those to the written collection. You'll find the stories behind the poems in a section at the back of the book.

This collection was written during the 1980s, when I was in my twenties, a turbulent time in my personal life. I was working as a teacher at Coedcae Comprehensive School, Llanelli, Wales: a school tough enough to be challenging (and that was just the staff).

Many of the poems were accepted by journals (listed in the acknowledgements) but my biggest breakthrough was via *The National Poetry Foundation* and its editor, Johnathon Clifford. I submitted six poems at a time to him and he kept those he deemed worthy of publication by the NPF as a collection. Some were published en route in the NPF journal *Pause*. Johnathon was appreciative, supportive and blunt.

I remember one poem came back with the note, 'You're talking to your belly button.' He had strong preferences. Some subjects were automatically out (including cats and religion). He was a fine poet himself, with an ear for editing poetry – and the confidence to do so. He suggested changes – a word here, a cut there – and they were good suggestions.

I have kept the order of the poems as he chose to print the first edition in 1988 but they are not in chronological order as written, so the stories behind them will be interwoven.

Poems are not puzzles to be solved. They are treasure chests. I hope these stories add riches rather than answers.

TO SECRETARY SANDRA'S GOLF-BALL

Your type has set the image of
The School's official missives,
dictating rigorous policies and
deleting all expletives,
but after Form One's verses,
even worse, their tasteless jokes –
I'm sure your cogs can cope
with all my poetry evokes.

WATCHING OLD PEOPLE

There must be easier pastimes
than this slow Chinese drip
into contempt by strip-light,
gauging women's ages by rings
on necks, round eyes, on fingers –
pale dragons hoarding gaudy
compensation for decline.

Inside each toughened epiderm
is its baby, toes bath-wrinkled
blinking yellow eyes at a strange world.
Only death peels skin-layers back
to egg shell fragility, till
some quintessence shines through.
Then you see kinder ways to watch.

MEN?

My little boy, who's only three,
says he's a man and don't need me;
all of my life, these big, strong men
have not needed me, again and again.

NOTHING PERSONAL

Worm-like, you burrow blindly
into any accommodating hole,
earthed in the blood-beat.

Then, rejecting the cooled heart
of your temporary refuge, you
shrivel, puckering in the light.

Less than worm, self-insufficient,
yet too easily detached,
translating into words only
'Thank you, hole, for being available.'

THE ARAN JUMPER

He left when I'd just set the pattern;

I didn't think he meant it,
called, 'Wait till the end of the row'
and heard the door close, quietly.

Strange. I'm not superstitious but
I always knit the pearl rows quicker
just in case. And that's when he left.

Like missing cracks in pavements which
I suppose is easier in size threes.
Tens his were. Are. Stretching across

whole paving stones and daring the cracks.
We seem to be through with skipping and covering.
I wasn't even listening, I was thinking

yarn forward and cable, orderly blue growth.
He chose the colour too. I've tried
to carry on but I keep missing stitches.

Somehow, he kept the pattern set.

SPRING PRAYER

Is it not very beautiful, oh my Lord,
very beautiful
like the first sleeveless shimmer of sun on sea ...

How can hearts bear without breaking, oh my Lord,
without breaking,
like the ebb-froth-flow pulsing the beach ...

Why rake us reluctant to spring-tides, oh my Lord,
to spring-tides
of juice pounding seeds through sweet bruised flesh ...

Why rend intellect tender to purest response, oh my Lord
purest response,
like the honeyed tilt of petals in a bee-borne breeze ...

Grant only dilution in rainbows, oh my Lord,
in rainbows,
reflecting life's close in each dew-drop.

PANDORA'S BOX

Pandora's box is too small,
once emptied of bloated evils.

How can you believe its promise
of puppies in spring?

Optimist, paint clouds in prison,
deny from heaven the deaths

that trail from honeyed woods.
You eat, unwitting, maggots

with your apple; you can't spit out
this serpent at your core.

Don't shut your cell-lid! Tiny
in your opium shelter

you'll miss the beauty of scales shed
to fall as petals in our garden.

INTEGRITY

Daddy plays his hi-fi,
Mummy just hears music;

Baby bites her nails to shreds,
jumps in boring boyfriends' beds,

wonders why she once was shy –
links lost, all fragmented.

Separate, disintegrate,
then find out when it's all too late,

soul's sweat is body's weight;
we think distinctions we create.

BIRTHDAY PRESENT FOR MY FATHER

We planned some sort of celebration
before we knew how serious it was,
how little chance you'd reach the date,
be seventy.
I thought so hard of presents,
wondered if to name a star would do,
some London scheme – an 'astral agency'.

Harder headed people said they'd sell me
two per cent of ocean, discount price,
to make your name immortal. Yet,

perhaps I wasn't so naïve; what proof
you're not returned to air and water,
birthday gifts conferred, though not by me?

NEVER FORGET YOUR WELSH

Sinews tensed and arms unsheathed from working sleeves,
miners swing on gates and lean by garden walls
on sunny sloping streets.

Today, the gossip
flies more carefully than usual; some had liked the boy
and had told his father so, or meant to
when his eyes spat tears.

Proud that man was as he walked to claim the tools
his boy had cared for, owned and lived by;
proud in grief and hiding bitter, pointless 'ifs'.

'If he'd been there, spoken some key word,
that self-inflicted death from mental wound
might not have happened.

'If his son's dour work-mates had been open
to his pain – instead they'd called him 'Saes',
exiled him by language from the country he thought his.

Only when he'd found the boy's tools missing, stolen,
did the father break; he said
'I'm Welsh as you are, valleys all my life
just like my son.'

In proof he poured out, line by perfect line
the Lord's prayer in their mother tongue
(all that he knew and in that all, himself).
'Can any of you here say this like me?'

No answer, but the tools appeared. He left.
Hanging over gates at dusk, in groups, the men
scuff hobnail boots and kick the silence dead.

TRIVIAL PURSUITS?

I believe in little gods of spite
who ice your paths and trip you up,
just when you're singing, feeling right.

I've learnt to value what I have,
hold onto now, not look ahead,
for if your future's sketched in rose
it's guaranteed to be duck-dead.

A cancelled booking, faithless man,
or bitchy workmates and slug clotted soil
spoil week-ends away, love-life or job
and shrubs bought as 'outstanding foil',

so when I die think only this of me;
a little god is what I've trained to be.

RE. GENERATION

HOW DARE YOU
try to alter views
I've taken thirty years to shape,
articulate, make mine!

Your spark is two hours old
to someone else's flame,

your pearls of wisdom
grit thrown in my eyes.

I cannot spare the energy
to wonder if you're right.

EQUALITY

My twelve-year-old pupils tell me
I could not be a taxi-driver –
I'd get raped because
I'm only a woman.

Waiting for the moderator of oral exams,
candidates' nerves grew
till, reassured, they heard
it was only a woman.

'Positive' laws protect me,
enforce my committee place,
my management job (one in four) because
I'm only a woman.

A man has problems too but
my question can't be answered;
how would a normal person feel
if *he* were only a woman?

'LAST LESSON' – BUT WORSE!

Please let me out.

There is no light here
where I strain to see
through blank, uncomprehending pupils,
alien minds.

Life narrows to this red-ant crawl,
Self-flagellation on an unresponsive sheet,
where I subject their adolescent insecurities
to my cold discipline of form.

COMMISSIONED WORK FOR MR PUDNER

I feel date-stamped
like half-price supermarket cheese
past 'sell-by'.
Did they call it AIDS because you scream for help
when the coin comes down tails?
(You've seen the warning poster.)
Chance! The chance of a life-time.
What if I misjudge this gap or close my eyes and choose
a less un-nerving death, crumpled on this road?
My dear ones would receive their Christmas presents,
salvaged from the wreckage,
bagged and tagged 'from the police'.
No explanations from me,
no time to face together,
as we've always done,
the truth, so often harsh.

I will say to him, How I was affected,
I don't know – as more and more will say.
We'll risk a look and smile at trusting,
sure of each other, sure as well
our daughters will assume soap-operas
of flurried infidelities.
He will need to be alone,

to practise being brave for me
and I must show his courage to the girls.

Death I can meet
but dying sounds dirty –
I need new clothes for that.
Dungarees I think, bright red.

And while I still can dash
along a beach, turn cartwheels in the spray
and spin the clouds around,
the life in me will fight the needles.
I would like us to go to the mountains again.
I'll tell him when I get home.

DEFECTIVE SYSTEM

–up the U.S.A.! Russian violinist defects!
Slavic cheekbones, tall, gauche, twenty,
pleased, though shy, to tell the Western world
to live here is a dream come true.

Another country's dream-green grass
(she'd heard of long ago)-
artistic freedom, always the
Mickey Mouse she'd longed to see,
be a concert star, solo defector.
(Tell the people dear, what instrument you play.)

'Mama,' (straight-faced) to the camera)
'of course I miss you!' (embarrassed, sub-titled)
'Remember they are listening...'
They? Soviet spies watch American T.V.?
At least they documentate in private.

'Mama I'm so happy here... I feel
I belong. I've joined the Exiles Club.
We're all so happy here...'
'Don't cry...'
'Send Katya my regards. Send–

POET DREAMS

Some Peter Pan land where the lost poets roam,
their fluttering images dreamed far from home
wake you at night with a vision of grandeur –
by morning you wish you had cuddled your panda
and slept to refresh those debauched, wrinkled eyes,
foreseeing you'll be at least old if not wise.

TUNISIAN COMPROMISE

Make me price.

Okay. Your country still festers in dark ages;
we'll apply tourism to your sores of poverty,
turn your land of red rock and bible shepherds
into a shimmering site of honeycombed concrete.

To feed your hives we'll bring the deutschmarks and
U.S. dollars, ex-oh-so-colonial French
for your mockery and casual over-charging;
even clumsy English with their trusting bonhomie
like optimistic oak trees poking roots
through shifting sands; cheap Christian alcohol
and even cheaper women for your drones. Still more!
In privacy we pledge protection – guns and bombs ...

You joke! No serious price!

Okay. Throw in the cure for camel-spit
and half a dozen fags.

Is good price! Tunisia will smile for cameras.

FOR MEMBERS OF F.A.*

Some time on a bible beach he said
'Go and be fishers of men ...'

You'll see by the trace of a blush
on her face, she's fishing again!

For complimentary tickets
her act scans quite a range –

fluffy jumpers, bawd games and
borrowed talk of social change.

Quite pretty, fairly bright, distinguished
only by this trite obsession;

to hear she is what she is not –
superlatives delay depression.

**Fishers anonymous – a society to help those addicted
to compliments to the detriment of family life.*

STUDY IN GREY

Dirt slants rain-wise, cross-hatching window panes,
smirching views of bean-poles counter-crossed;
slates grey, skies slate, in dull reflections of
oppressive regulations. Whorling in
warm mouthed mist, a tentative finger
drawlingly defies with parabola
the straightness of a glass partitioned world.

Seeking silver, lost mercurial argent,
she withdraws through lucent eyes, mourning still
deep pools ringed with irises and fine crushed
petals of bitter geranium blood.

Once night had drawn her, tear by wintry tear,
rainswept up to Llangedeyrne mountain
where mist met limestone, scarping, shelving, steep
again to crux of stone rings, truly wed
in ancient token to the gods of earth.

We are grown unsure of our ground; the act
of kneeling brings us down too close to worms
and worship bred in bourgeois bleat-barns
smacks Victorian of hypocrisy. Still,
she knelt and knew pure grit of wet stone
jarring flesh colder, then fevered warm.

No miracles;
just cloud-break clearing thirty seconds moonlight
to glow unearthly on her outstretched arm.
Small shifts of feeling clear awareness till
all greys rain diminutions of silver.

DEFINED BY LOSS

Most wives are widows one day,
statistically. I too might know
the bathroom sink clean and hairless;
the cacti that won't grow;

empty space where useful shelves
might once have been erected;
empty nights, no warmth, no talk,
alone now, lost, neglected.

The ageing tread of feet on stairs
is mine, the fear of falling.
At wake of day a trim-phone ring,
a neighbour's kind 'alive-check' call-in.

No point, no point – there never was –
but once days needed you so much
to kiss them better, make a home,
you didn't sit and crave one touch.

FARMERS SHOOT FIRST

Lamb-spring in the valleys and
prayed-for green predominates,
freshening one sun-shot day
with avocado shadows.

Shades of winter linger white
in crinkled dog-hair, but rugs
by firesides lose their warmth when
mud spawns and blood quickens.

Sprung through hedges not yet thickened,
ears miming deafness, daftness, all
excuse, she followed sheep-like
the fellowship of the fields.

Now her blood feeds lamb-skips; mere
hairs on carpet and old crap
on the lawn confirm a life.
Spring is the season of dead dogs.

ARTHUR'S PLEA

My son embodies my own faults; like him
I had ideals for which I hacked off heads –
yes, and severed wives who broke my laws.

Incestuous concentrate of kingly
arrogance, he cannot change his nature.
When this truth came home I cried to Merlyn,

'Bitter black this day has been!' He answered,
'A day Sire, just like any other, but tainted
black and bitter by your mood. Be grateful!

Few men know their own seeds of destruction,
yet fate shows all men death in their sons' eyes;
our children's future always post-dates ours.'

The generation, yes, but not the man;
Mordred, still-born as I wished, will not live
much beyond my death, his end fulfilled. Forgive
us both for what he is about to do.

NOTE FROM GUINEVERE TO LANCELOT

I am your Excalibur; take me and
burn the fatal letters from my future.
Fire-brand me new tempered, forged through melting.
trusty, ringing true. Perhaps I would be

but the letters of the past cannot be
burnt so cleanly, not though their owner
fans the flames. Tatters would lurk in corners,
dirtied shadows of our young selves.

No, I can't live with you. No hurt to others
will I cause to cut with double blade.
The time will come to cast me away.

LANCELOT INSANE

I'm free. I choose banquets of poached nettles
and rowanberries as jewels in my beard.

No allegiances, no double-bind of trust betrayed.
Free as a bird ...
No longer hawk to stoop at king's command,
nor gold-finch glimmering in sociable flights,

but stone-chat croaking as it skims the heath.
It is enough to see the gorse blossom.
Does even nature's gold need lance and spur?
Tributes of blood to make the season's wine

taste delicate? And sweet. Like ...
Look – reed blades quivering! This surely is
enough. The very grass is quick, hurling
a song skywards to distract the stranger

from the nest. The refuge I call home shows
alarming tendencies to carve features
half-forgotten in its stone; there that curve
traced by speedwell, surely ...

Three years my shield has barred the entrance to
this cave, its device tarnished from hiding.
I've chewed sorrel long enough; I've nothing
new to learn from bitterness alone.

Together they call me and I will go
between them again, kneeling ...
My lord, your knight, and oh my lady, yours.

A NIGHT AT THE THEATRE

i)
Choose your poison, tragedy queen,
before the flaked paint shows your drying tears;
clasp asp, sip limpet lips –
drain all unpronounceable lexic possibilities.
We writhe with you, dears,
positively achieve catharsis together;
emotional drag's the queen for me.

ii)
Sceptics, seated at the front, see
Banquo's ghost crawl the whole table's length
to make a breathless apparition;
see flutters in the wings –
stage-born gaits and gestures, fabulous as phoenix,
dwindling to the ashes of a nervous cigarette;
hear, tickling the resentful hush of death believed,
miraculous sighs exhaled by corpses;
till, touching purses, tickets, buttons,
all more real than people,
they fumble towards the neon sign
where the street performance begins,
disbelief irrevocably suspended.

TO BLUEBEARD
FROM THE WOMAN WHO DOES FOR HIM

Sorry sir.
I heard the children singing.
'Bluebeard hangs his maiden-heads
all round his walls;
we hope the next one that he weds
will squash his fun, his fun, his fun ...'

Not being in the wife line myself,
I thought I'd tidy your room, your locked room.
Isn't that what you wanted when
you warned me and showed me the key?

I'm not averse, I own, to
a peek, a poke a pry.
Clumsy I am; you'll have to mend the lock,
if locks you want still.
But that's the point –
why lock a room
simply furnished, clean and cosy,
empty only of a woman's touch?

Then I saw those women on the walls,
Helen of Troy to Shelley Long ...
too much for me, that gallery of vogues.
Turning to go, I noticed then the muddy footprints
– mine.
All dirt and damage in that room
I'd brought in with me.

So much you gave, too much you asked,
perhaps, sir?

AFTER THE MEXICAN EARTHQUAKE, 1985

They see me huddled in blankets,
cradling this stone and think me mad,
but God will keep his bargain this time.
It's like the children's game,
'Baby, scissors, stone;
stone, scissors, baby.'
Close your hand and hide your hope.

Giving birth was like nothing foreseen.
If it was worse, I do not remember it,
but that it was better, yes, I remember that.
Earth-shaking.
No-one laughs now at fingers crossed,
averting words' witchcraft.

The earth shook. Another minor world disaster
dropped walls ten feet thick around my son.
Babies being smothered in wombs
as dark and cosy as their mothers'.
This is the sixth day; we who remain
have seen nineteen rebirths.

At the first, such gladness – as if your own,
or promise of.
At ten the rate slowed; we remembered the odds.
Twelve was dead.
How cold and high the forceps, excavating rubble,
how deadly tired the man in charge,
wondering when to say all hope was cruel.

Pillars in the landscape, we mothers of stone.
Sing to me, little stone, I love you.
Keep my milk flowing.

Twenty-three was mine, alive, my breach birth.
Remembering husband, family, I see them again.
Were they with me all that wait?
I look back at mothers huddled in blankets;
less hard to give birth to a stone
than be crushed by a void.

MERRY- GO-ROUND

Ask me another, darling,
ask me another, dear,
but don't ask me whether I love you –
not now, not next week, not this year!

So there's another, darling,
so there's another, dear,
and you assume I will still love you
and not say I don't want you near.

Don't tell my mother, darling,
please don't tell the neighbours, dear,
and I will pretend that I love you –
we'll patch it with babies and beer.

You're starting to smother me, darling,
you're faded and boring, my dear.
It's my turn to play with another
and your turn alone with your fear.

WHICH CLUB ARE YOU IN?

If I wore my Brownie badges, would all
and only other Brownies speak to me?
Saying 'I'm a Brownie too,'
or, 'I was,' or, 'I would like to be.'
United in our Browniehood we'd stand,
whatever our taste in literature.

Instead I push a pram
and all the coo-ers coo-ee to me
and all the others don't,
I'm transparent to men
who used to look twice
and I can see right through
them.

DUET

There's a button missing from your shirt,
revealing the hair-gold smoothness
I hurried to reach;
why have you not replaced it?

There is a button missing, as you say,
but this is not the shirt I wore that day.

There's a beige card stamped 'Non-fiction'
far from the feminine fuss of
its handbag compartment;
why have you not returned it?

The library ticket – I used it once, I know.
but lost it over eighteen months ago.

There's a pet-name unspoken,
hiding behind a common-place of
jaded familiarity;
why have you not re-cycled it?

That pet-name I have used with great success
on girls who values their quick pleasures less.

There's rosemary and rue, grown from seed,
there's catmint for my dead black tom –
I loved him too.
You see those chives, called everlasting?

Your cat is dead – so what? Don't make a fuss,
don't cry and pout and take it out on us.
We've had some fun – you're quite good in the sack,
apart from moaning you get nothing back.

And if by chance you grow a seed of mine,
tell him from me he comes of super
-ficial line.

THE THREE WISE MONKEYS

One monkey saw two fresh-faced kids
throw a scabby mongrel from Floor 3
of Tesco's multi-storey car-park.
While old owner cried, unbalanced,
and police appealed for witnesses,
it closed its eyes.

Monkey two came slurring out 'The Nag's Head',
swinging its tail and glad of some fresh air.
It heard a girl scream, 'Help!'
a scuffle somewhere in the dark.
It covered ears, went home to bed
and hid from TV, radio, papers
which all told where and how she'd died

Monkey three, observant neighbour.
sees cigarette burns on babies' arms,
hears nightmares knocking on its wall,
says nothing; not involved in outcomes
long predicted which twist our future
in their tortured grip.

Monkeys are better survivors then people.

A BAD DAY,
TECHNOLOGICALLY SPEAKING

Musing on an evening out, she drives her Toyota
so fast round a 5/8□ curve
the needle breaks on a careless pin. Shit!

Somewhere a brown girl carries water from the well.

The radio spreads typhoid and race wars;
impatiently she twists the dial and scrapes
the paintwork on a newly varnished nail. Shit!

Elsewhere a brown girl carries water from the well.

Dressed to kill, she clears her palate with
due consideration of others' deprivation,
conscious only comfortably that

everywhere there's shit in the wells.

Y X X?

This is no matter fit for metre,
so let me write in doggerel or worse,
then those embarrassed by the subject
can criticise to prude's content the verse.

I'm gay – O.K.? – you must have heard,
for square pegs, round holes, Mum's the word.
But Freud most modern thought decries,
condemning his simplistic lies.

Romantics cite us Plato's view
of souls embodied sharing two
imperfect selves to make one whole.
Hearing the spheres sing barcarole,

should lovers stop advances tender
to check appendices of gender?
These silly, trite appurtenances
serve sweetly subject to love's dances

when we ensure component parts bear
true relation to our hearts where
integrity demands a blend
of warmest lover, closest friend.

Enough of romance – I prefer
more honest reasons why I 'err'.
Gaze in narcissistic pool
and swear you could not, would not fool

with beauties mirrored to display
your own potential, cloned this way;

or, post-teen rebel, choose to miss
the staid delights of hetero kiss,

preferring nights in dubious bars
to life-long T.V., kids' catarrhs.
Object to this, say coupledom
is common source of joy? To some.

You sigh, 'I'm glad she married me';
observe this bond in homo parody,
generalized, no-one denies,
but wrists are slit by marriage ties.

My motives, mixed, are as perverse
as nature's over-flowing purse
of varied coinage, base or gold
when stamped in current values' mold.

So read this camp or read this straight,
to you, my reader, I relate.

THE LADY AND THE MINSTREL

You claim the challenge of chess;
so be it, with my lord away,
the prize my bed this coming night,
depending on how well you play.
You laugh and say I've lost the game –
discovered check or some such trick –
but look! At my queen's side her loving
knight protects to the death;
her kin led out his men to war
and sacrificed no pawn or rook
while bishops parleyed first for peace.
This one brave knight threw down the glove
but scorned the serpent's forked attack
and, trapped, took two for one.
Your king skulks in his castle while
your queen pursues my men; your knights
are sheltered by doomed pawns – killing
is done by bishops' transverse thrust.
Say whose tactics were more skilled, whose
game better suited to the stake?
Some aptitude you've shown for play;
from these brave chequered lives you make
romantic strategies, not chess.
Be at my side when I awake.

i) YOUNG LOVE

To you, my sweet, I fondly gave
a winter lover's purest rose –
blush-pink cheeks, sparkling eyes
and a terribly runny nose.

It is the flu, it is the flu
that streams from me to breed in you.

Then came the spring and more than bees
felt nature's call to pollinate;
we tested several grassy banks
and now you're three weeks late.

Give love its due, there's more than flu
that streams from me to breed in you.

ii) NOT JUST MARRIED

If only I had liked you less
or you my husband more –
we'd not have started that caress
which finished on the floor.
And now the fun is over, 'dear'
or has it just begun?
Were we both being quite sincere
in swearing, 'Just the one ...'?
And is it, 'Come to my house' now
'No, mine, the wife's away,'
(and spread the word around somehow,
we might as well all play).
From time to time you feel a qualm,
and wonder if we should?
Just run your nails along my arm
and tell me that I'm good.

iii) LEAVE IN SILENCE

We tend to excess
in airing our grievances,
addictive process
of unsavoury appearances
in print, on T.V.
whining, 'if he'd just
talked to me!'
'She drank so! She fussed!'
A modern documentary,
U.S. of course
portrays all contemporary
sins of divorce;
'Nothing folks is left unsaid'
no blood, sweat, sperm stains,
snuggling in bed,
shroud the couple's remains.
Switching off, admit
some admiration for the few
who quit
in silence and with tears too.

The Stories Behind the Poems

To Secretary Sandra's Golf-Ball

In the days before word processors, the school secretary, Sandra, typed up my first poems as a favour for me, on the highly modern electric typewriter with a type element that rotated before striking, a 'golf ball'. I liked the idea of my slightly daring poetry brushing ink with official school missives. A whiff of the illicit.

Watching Old People

Most other players in the bridge club were in their sixties and older. I was by far the youngest, in my early twenties, and I observed the human hands, not just the cards. Gnarled, the diamond patterns of skin ever more like scales, and decorated by large jewellery, these ageing hands reminded me of dragons, with their legendary taste in hoards of gold. My youthful disgust at the ageing process turned into fascination with the layers that make up a human, not just skin, and then to the conclusion that there are *'kinder ways to watch'*. I'm rather keen on jewellery myself, now, and I don't mind turning into a dragon.

Men?

When my son was going through one of his rebellious phases, at about three years old, I heard him singing in the bathroom, *'Men are the best, I don't need you.'* That made me think about the men in my past, their tough exteriors and how vulnerable they really were.

Nothing Personal

I really needed to say to a man, *'You're a prick.'* So I wrote it instead and it was published in *Envoi*. For some reason that still makes me feel good. We're quits.

The Aran Jumper

Knitting has been a form of meditation for me at different times in my life. When on honeymoon at twenty, I bought sea-blue Aran wool on a Scottish island, and knitted a suitably complicated cable jumper for my husband. As the marriage unravelled, I tried to hold on. I imagined him leaving me and the destruction of the pattern we'd made. But I was the one who left.

Spring Prayer

At a low point in my life, I remember being at the local beach, in Llanelli, Wales, and watching the waves, the rhythm of the tide. Nature and landscapes have always brought me a sense of calm, of a bigger universe in which I am a little, temporary sparkle of life. Although an atheist, the rhythms of my Christian upbringing stay with me and the chorus in this poem is spiritual, like a black American spiritual, rather than sectarian. The jump from spirituals to the blues is easily crossed and it is that music, its repetition and its pattern, that I felt in this poem. Battered by too much passion, seeking reasons, and finding them in the pulse of the tide, in a bee's flight, in a rainbow.

Pandora's Box

In the Greek myth, Pandora opened her box (a jar in the original versions) and unloosed evils on a perfect world. She closed it too late to keep anything in the box but hope. What if we *live* in a sort of Pandora's box? Would life be wonderful without the 'evils' of disease, despair, death? Do optimists even see such evils and is it better if you don't?

I've always loved the line, *'Optimists paint clouds in prison,'* and that was my first choice as the title of this book. I remember watching a documentary where a prisoner did just that. Years later, my uncle wrote his WW2 memoir of being a POW and that's what he did, in solitary confinement. He read and drew on the walls to keep himself from getting bored. It's strange the way life connects with literature, after the words are already written.

A friend who was a student of mine in the 80s reminded me recently that he and his classmates asked me what I thought was the meaning of life. The easy answer for a young teacher would have been '42' as *The Hitch-hiker's Guide to the Galaxy* was a hit then. Instead, I said, *'Puppy-dogs in springtime.'* That stayed in his mind for over thirty years and he tracked me down via social media to continue the discussion.

That's still as close as I'll ever get to 'the meaning of life' so I stick by that. Although the poem points out that you don't always get your puppy-dogs, hope remains in the box with you. And you have to accept the beauty, the dark and the light, intertwined. That's how it is. Like the serpent in the Garden of Eden – Eden was never 'good'. The serpent was there too.

Integrity

When my father bought hi-fi, he spent hours considering whether the woofers were better on one set of speakers than another, as he tested them. It was fun to join in and discuss the technical details. My mother had no interest in 'sound quality' but loved music, and I think I am more like her. That split of appreciation between music and sound made me think of other splits, where the mechanics is separated from emotion, as in casual sex.

Birthday Present for My Father

A love poem. My father died a month before his 70th birthday and all our plans for a special birthday had been dropped months before, when we realised that there would be no recovery from cancer this time. The internet was new at this time but, before the terminal diagnosis, I did find unusual presents online, and I was attracted to the idea of naming a star after him (despite some mockery at the idea). *George* would have been an unusual name for a star. I was less impressed at an offer to sell me a portion of ocean as a gift for a loved one. As I see it, we all return to stardust, so the greater universe chose those final gifts.

Never Forget Your Welsh

I was on 'shush' duty behind the scenes of the annual school musical, when one of the local adult actors joined me in the dressing-room. He was playing a circus-style strongman, and seemed a jolly character, probably in his fifties. The pupils all headed out on stage and he started talking to me.

He poured out the whole story. How his son spoke no Welsh, felt isolated 'down the mines', became more depressed than anyone realised, and committed suicide. How the father went to the mine to claim his son's tools, but they'd been stolen and nobody would look at him. How he recited 'The Lord's Prayer' in Welsh, the only Welsh he knew, and told them he and his son were as Welsh as they were. He told me how much it hurt. Then it was his turn on stage and I didn't see him again. But I told his story for him.

The title is the slogan from a beer advert in the 70s but here it is ironic, a reminder of the language war zone that is Welsh v English, a war in which I have close friends on both sides.

Trivial Pursuits

Playing on the name of the popular board game, I wanted to record the trivial pursuits of 'the little gods of spite'. I find it very easy to picture these malicious imps, like Puck and the fairies in *A Midsummer Night's Dream,* who take pleasure in petty acts of destruction. They are responsible for the little things that go wrong and they are still at work. How else could errors appear in the final version of a book that has been professionally edited and checked a dozen times? It's them. The little gods of spite. And what a great afterlife that would be, to become one.

Re. Generation

One of the children phoned up to announce a change of university course, motivated by a desire to do good in the world. The prospect horrified my husband, John, but he was the epitome of calm support while on the phone and then exploded afterwards. How much of the 'generation gap' comes because we hold to opinions that have taken time and pain to form? Do any of us want to re-think, when faced with something we disagree with completely? The family clash never happened; that course wasn't chosen. But the question re generation remains. Isn't that the job of the next generation? Doesn't regeneration come from change?

Equality

Many of my poems deal with gender, sex discrimination and assumptions about what's normal. Yes, all these examples of sex discrimination did happen, and a lot more. My pupils *did* tell me I couldn't be a taxi-driver because I'd get raped.

The list of things I was told that women couldn't do was too long to bother trying to remember. When I succeeded at these things, I was unfeminine, *'behaving like a man'*: Catch 22.

The positive discrimination was as bad as the negative. There was supposed to be one female among four senior managers in a school. Too often, this meant a woman manager who had no training in curriculum or timetabling, so she was in charge of pastoral care and sanitary towels. Don't get me wrong - I do think pastoral care is important but the managers who became Headteachers were those who also understood curricula and timetables!

I'm very proud that I was the first woman to be a secondary Headteacher in Wales. Marina in Ceredigion was appointed at the same time, so we share both the honour and the sexist irritations.

Last lesson – but worse

The quotes around 'Last Lesson' in the title, refer to D.H. Lawrence's poem of that name, about one of THOSE lessons every teacher hates. This is my awful-last-lesson poem. All teachers have some bad lessons and bad days, when you face *'blank uncomprehending pupils'*. I like the double-meaning in 'pupils' and remember looking into my students' eyes, finding only hostility. You had to fight hard to win them over but you understood where they came from. They were only protecting themselves. Sometimes, magic happened.

Commissioned Work for Mr Pudner

The Pudner twins, Jeremy and Damian, were two lively students, who were in my chess club, and in the team that went through several rounds of the Sunday Times Chess Competition. This was a big achievement as the competition was dominated by private schools.

The twins were also in my English class. As I recall, Damian complained about a homework I set so I said that if he did my task, I'd write one he set for me. He demanded a poem about having AIDS. This was probably in revenge for me emphasizing 'empathy' in preparation for the GCSE exam taken by sixteen-year-olds. So I wrote a poem about having AIDS and I read it to the class. Hence the title.

Defective System

I watched a Russian violinist talking about her defection to the USA in a news item meant to show how happy she was and how wonderful the USA is, how free she was now. I saw mixed messages and contradictions. I saw a girl who knew what she was supposed to say and now had two sets of watchers instead of one. Censorship is not always overt and you are often 'free' only if you stay inside your box. Censorship can be fear of the consequences if you don't – even if there are no consequences. You should read this poem twice as the end leads to the beginning, to make you think again.

Poet Dreams

Where does my writing come from? I admit that I have strange dreams. I've never taken illegal drugs because my imagination is wild enough without them and I used to have terrible nightmares. Writers are allowed to have visions and hear voices without being considered mentally ill. I'm glad this is so but I do wonder why. What makes the difference?

Tunisian Compromise

I holidayed in Tunisia in 1983 and was overwhelmed by confusion as to whether I was doing good or ill to such a place by being there as a tourist. I found it threatening to be grabbed and dragged into a shop; tiring to haggle over buying anything. I found it daunting to watch out for thieves and to avoid beggars. The hotels were safe places (ironic nowadays!) in which to recover, amidst fake 'traditional' entertainment and an air of contempt.

There were three sets of starting prices on the streets; for Germans (most expensive) for French and for British tourists. I spoke French so could communicate but learned to switch to English if I was buying something. I made friends with our waiter, who offered to take me and my (first) husband out for the evening, on his night off. He took us to a disco, at a different hotel. I danced with my husband and I danced with the waiter. He asked for a photo of me with him. I did wonder what he was going to do with it but obliged. Maybe his 'British girlfriend' was worth kudos or even money in some strange situation I could only imagine.

Everything felt like that, as if I was missing the point of some seedy barter. Like a wise traveller, I kept my shoulders and knees well-covered but, even so, I felt ill-at-ease. There are glances that let you know you are out of your cultural depth. I felt as if I'd done something wrong but I didn't know what it was. I haggled successfully for a camel-hair coat, with a hood, and embroidery round the seams. When I wore it to meet my fellow-teachers for a drink at the pub in Llanelli, they said they could smell me coming in the door. I loved it. I was good at not fitting in. Lots of practice from an early age.

For Members of F.A.

An irreverent quote from Jesus' words, *'I will make you fishers of men.'* When I write a poem in the first person, it's usually somebody else's story; when it's in the third person, it might well be about me. This one is about me. I like compliments. Who doesn't? I have been known to fish for them. I was once told off at the bridge club by a lovely lady in her seventies, who said to me, *'You don't need to fish for compliments, you know!'* But I still do, sometimes.

Study in Grey

I'd spent all day sewing curtains, and the endless straight lines had made me understand the term 'hemmed-in'. The non-view out the window didn't help. Wales is grey. It rains in the summer, it rains in the winter and I lived up a hill, in the mist. I felt restless and angry at the world, and late in the evening, maybe 11.00pm, I took my reluctant dog for protection and walked up to Mynydd Llangenderyne.

This is one of my favourite places and it features in my novel, *No Bed of Roses*. Broody in daylight: in pitch black the standing stones and ridges are mythic. I didn't dare scramble far across the heath as some of the bogs were treacherous. When the moon suddenly appeared, the silver shimmer changed the landscape and my mood. Grey and silver; different ways of seeing. Everything is given form by the light shed on it.

Defined by Loss

My father died in 1986 and I saw my mother become a widow, saw the changes in her life. She was side-swiped by the small things. He loved growing cacti, would sing a wordless *'Tra-la-la'* while he watered them from his little yellow watering can (one teaspoon each on Wednesday and Sundays, he told my sister). When he was in hospital with a cancer scare, a dress-rehearsal in Spring 86, I took him a cactus in a china boot, instead of flowers, with a little card, *'To the Old Boot.'* That's how love was expressed, from me to him. Whether it was the singing or the watering, the cacti no longer thrived after his death and my mother gave up on them. *Widow* became her new identity.

Farmers Shoot First

The saying is, 'Shoot first, ask questions later.' This is what Welsh farmers do when they see a dog in a field of sheep. This is what a Welsh farmer did when he shot and killed my dog. Bianca was the dog I'd waited for all my young life, a 'deaf' Pyrenean Mountain Dog, who turned out to be traumatised but not deaf.

We adopted her when she was seven months old, because I saw an advert for a deaf Pyrenean up for adoption and knew this was the dog for me. She'd been bought as a puppy by some family 'down south in England' and sent back to the breeder 'because she was deaf'. At first, I couldn't believe that she heard me but at last I accepted that it wasn't my imagination. She was a sweet, gentle dog and, when she was about a year old, at Christmas, she had a collie puppy as a present. She tolerated that puppy dangling from her chin by its teeth till she was scarred, and she never hurt the little one.

In the springtime, she escaped from the garden, twice, following a Jack Russell who lived up the road, into the fields. After she'd escaped the second time, a policeman called, with her collar, to tell me she'd been in a field with sheep and the farmer had shot her dead. I felt like I was the one who'd been shot. The grief and shock and *unfairness* crippled me. The Jack Russell had returned home safely. I checked and neither of them had hurt any sheep – the shooting was precautionary. Of course. Pyrenean Mountain Dogs have been bred for centuries to protect sheep. I've been owned by six of them, and wrote my understanding of them into my book *Someone to Look Up To*.

My grief exploded all the barriers I'd built at university. My degree in English Literature had convinced me that literature was written by great, dead men and I'd stopped writing at eighteen. Reading Stevie Smith when I was twenty-two had opened my eyes to possibilities but when I lost Bianca, I wrote my hurt into this poem. From this moment on, I was writing again. And it was personal. The universe could no longer be trusted.

Arthur's Plea

I've always loved the Arthurian legends, which I've read in many versions. I suspect they're part of the inspiration for my *Troubadours Quartet*. My favourite book as a teenager was *The Once and Future King* by T.H. White. The central 'eternal triangle', the heroic knight brought low by passion, Arthur's fatal begetting of Mordred, all sprinkled with magic dust and Merlin's prophesies – irresistible.

My portrayal of Arthur here is at the stage when he faces his adult son, knowing that Mordred will kill him and everything Camelot stands for. How do you feel at having given birth to the instrument of your death? When Arthur pleads for forgiveness, he is owning responsibility for his part in this classical tragedy.

Don't we all, as Merlin says in this poem, see our death in our children's eyes? The consequence of sex is death in biological terms – it's a reproduction system. Many creatures die on mating, their purpose fulfilled. Perhaps Arthur's fate is a brutal example of a universal truth.

It occurs to me that we often hear this debate in the news about mothers and their responsibility for sons who grow up to be killers; here it is the father who has 'engendered' his own destruction.

Note from Guinevere to Lancelot

This was the first poem I ever had accepted by a journal, *Outposts*. That first acceptance is an amazing moment. One editor told me he received 10,000 poems each week so rejection is not a sign that you should give up. But acceptance! By such a prestigious journal! It motivated me to keep writing. More of my poems were accepted by a variety of journals and I found Jonathon Clifford and *The National Poetry Foundation*.

From a few acceptances, to enough poems for my first book.

This was also one of the first poems I showed to anyone other than close friends. The well-known Welsh poet, Tony Curtis, was visiting my school to work with youngsters, and I asked him if he'd feed back on my work, He did and was positive, although he said Excalibur was more often a phallic symbol in poetry. Not in mine!

According to some tales, Excalibur had *'Take Me!'* engraved on one side of the blade and *'Throw Me Away!'* on the other. How would Arthur's wife react to her husband's sword? How would any woman in a passionate, doomed affair react to such a message? Guinevere knew from the first kiss that her love affair with Lancelot was doomed. To say, *'Take Me!'* is easy. To say, *'Throw me away!'* is harder and it is the promise made in the poem. The affair must end before any hurt is caused.

A poem of illicit, doomed love and the double blade of the collection's title. The hurt cuts both ways in any love affair started in full knowledge that it cannot continue. Not only adultery but class, culture, religion, age, illness can all write *'Throw me away!'* on one side of the blade. To know that, accept it and still follow such a passion, is both love and curse. There is a kind of courage in such a love.

Lancelot Insane

There is a period in the *Morte d'Arthur* when Lancelot goes insane, grows a wild beard and lives on the heath. Driven crazy by the impossible choice between his passion for Guinevere and his loyalty to his king (and friend), Arthur, he does the medieval equivalent of living 'off the grid.' I could see him on Mynydd

Llangedeyrne, among the gorse bushes and the stonechats. I too have tried to hide from choices I didn't want to make, and, like Lancelot, realised that hiding cannot last. His final words are an oath of loyalty to his king that is immediately broken by his oath of more than loyalty to his lady. He can't stay in hiding and he can't hold back from her.

A Night at The Theatre

I loved teaching Shakespeare and saw many plays at the theatre. In these two poems you can enjoy Cleopatra and Banquo from *'the Scottish play'*, with some camp acting, and play on the idea of catharsis and a climax. At one production, I did indeed see Banquo's ghost crawling along under the table before making his appearance. Those moments are the joys of live theatre!

To Bluebeard

This one will always make me laugh. I wrote it for my bridge partner, who'd married twice and who struck me as a perfectionist, looking for the perfect woman. So, in fun, I imagined him as Bluebeard, and that he let me into his closed room to see what all the rumours were really about. He was very keen on Shelley Long at the time so I stuck her head on the imaginary wall.

I played with words enough in this poem to make any reader dizzy. I borrowed the technique from rude ditties where the obvious rhyme is replaced with a tamer word, so 'fun' does not rhyme with 'walls.' If you read it aloud, I'm sure you can supply a suitable rhyme.

Maiden-heads is an obvious double meaning, derived from the story itself where Bluebeard has the heads of maidens on his walls. 'The woman who does for him' plays on the slang for a cleaner and at least three other meanings.

And, of course, I was 'not in the wife line' because we were both married. It was great fun to write and to read to him but the last joke was on me.

Dear reader, I married him. I am Wife Number 3. He still doesn't have a clue what the poem means so we'll keep it that way. After all, we've been together thirty-two years now.

After the Mexican Earthquake, 1985

On the news, I saw the Mexican women sitting, waiting, to see whether their new-born babies would be recovered from the wreckage of a maternity hospital, after a terrible earthquake. In writing about them, for the first time I expressed a little of how I felt about my miscarriages. I knew what it was like to be crushed by a void. I had three pregnancies in three nightmare years: two miscarriages and then the birth of my son in 1984.

One at a time, a baby was brought into daylight by the rescue workers and the work did indeed carry on for days, with babies still alive after six days. With *some* babies still alive. The newsreader said something like, 'the twelfth was dead,' or 'the twenty-third was alive' and all I could do was imagine how each baby's mother felt.

At the time of my miscarriages, I was unable to grieve properly, or to share my grief, and, on the surface, I functioned 'normally'. I have come to terms with those years, accepted my 'extreme' reactions and that for me there will always be two more children in my life than there are, regardless of how few months I was pregnant each time.

I find it hard to forgive the callous way I was treated in hospital. In a ward alongside pregnant women looking forward to their babies, I was told that I needed to miscarry a third time for it to be worth investigating. Luckily, a bridge friend was a midwife, took over my antenatal care, administered a weekly testosterone boost (who'd have thought I might be short of testosterone!) and my third pregnancy resulted in that everyday miracle, a baby. And I returned to the world, seeing it differently.

Merry-go-round

Every workplace has its liaisons and break-ups, and mine was no exception. My observation of others' marriages deepened my cynicism. It seemed to me that all marriages became shams enlivened by adultery, and the only question was how long it took before this happened. This poem is often taken as autobiographical because my marriage broke up, and perhaps it is, in showing my attitude. But not in any of the facts.

Which Club Are You In?

I remember saying to my then bridge partner, John, *'I'm having a baby, not a lobotomy.'* Once I became a mother, I was shocked at how people's attitude to me changed. Because I was pushing a pram, I was supposed to make friends with women who were mothers. Regardless of whether we had anything else in common – and I've never been interested in discussing babies. I don't even *like* other people's babies, although my own was perfection, and my love for him was instant, fierce, forever. I had to fight against happy-nappy-talk but luckily my (mainly childless) friends were capable of cuddling my baby and discussing politics at the same time. My main peer role model as a mother managed the care of two small children alongside an Open University degree in Physics, leading to a career as a top physicist, so I didn't think I was unusual.

Duet

Passion and break-up: love on one side and 'just sex' on the other, in a hurtful relationship. One person hoping always that behind the harsh words, there is deeper feeling. The cat is real, named Simone until I discovered she was a he and renamed him Simmy. He used to watch me and purr when I undressed, which I found extremely flattering. I was brought up to control emotion and I imagined others would react badly if I showed how much I cared. His death did hurt, and there were people around me cruel enough to tell me not to make such a fuss, but I don't think I ever risked those comments. I hid everything and imagined conversations that never happened; lived and imagined relationships that might have meant everything or might have meant nothing. And I had the last word in my poems.

The Three Wise Monkeys

I lived in Wakefield for a year and used to walk home from the railway station after a day's work in Leeds, past the prison, where the surveillance camera followed me along one side, until I turned the corner and into supposedly safer streets. One of the places I walked past, wasteland by *The Nag's Head*, was the scene of a rape, and I read in the local paper how the woman had screamed, been heard and was ignored. Witnesses realised afterwards what they had heard.

That's the story in the third verse and I remembered it when, years later, I read another story, in Llanelli, Wales, of children tormenting a dog in front of its old owner. In both cases, onlookers had kept away from trouble, turned a blind eye, not spoken out. That made me think of the proverbial three wise monkeys: *See no evil, hear no evil, speak no evil.* In my poem they are *not* wise. They might be *street*-wise and saving themselves but they are wrong!

In France, 'Non-assistance à personne en danger,' is a crime, and that seems right to me. This poem is a plea to act if you think somebody else is in danger. Where does turning a blind eye lead? *The only thing necessary for the triumph of evil is for good men to do nothing* – Edmund Burke.

A Bad Day, Technologically Speaking

A friend who worked for the U.N. has told me one of their sayings: *'The refugees wish they had our problems.'* The woman with the Toyota sewing-machine (me) swears at trivial irritations; for the brown girl, the shit is real.

From my teenage years, I used to make my own clothes and I always felt I was driving a fast car, sewing with the Toyota. I'd push that pedal down as hard as it would go.

I still feel guilty about the divide between rich and poor, between first and third world countries – 'comfortably' guilty because I have food, warmth and clean water, and a lot more!

I don't know why I often write about myself in the third person and about others in the first person. Maybe I need to distance myself to craft my own experiences into poetry, and to get closer to others to craft theirs.

YXX?

My brother 'came out' in the early 1980s and I wrote this poem for him, including some of the theories about why a man might be homosexual; an extra X chromosome, suffocating mother-son relationship, narcissism and so on. Or just love, that pays no attention to *'appendices of gender'*. The line, *'To you, my brother, I relate,'* is a Baudelaire reference (*'mon semblable, mon frère'*) but literal in this case, which amused me.

My brother enjoyed his poem but wished he hadn't received it just as he was taking a Law exam; he said he was puzzling it out when he should have been concentrating on legal questions.

I am not male and not homosexual (fact, not defence) but that first-person statement *'I'm gay'* had interesting consequences. I entered a selection of poems from this collection for a competition and received feedback to the effect that they were a sensitive exploration of a gay man's experiences. This was news to me. Because of this poem, the entire collection had been read as if in e.g. *Duet* the narrator is a gay man.

But why not? The starting point of my poems doesn't fix their interpretation, nor their resonance with the personal experience of the reader. I used to teach students that a first-person narrator is not necessarily the author. My standard lesson would begin, 'If a poem starts, *'Woof woof! Yummy kibble in my bowl!'* is it written by a golden retriever?' Of course, the students would say no, and we'd move on to more complex relationships between the author and the persona an author uses when writing in the first person. As a parting gift, one student wrote me a poem from her golden retriever persona – moments like that are treasures in a teacher's life.

The Lady and the Minstrel

As a keen chess player, and reader of medieval literature, I wondered about the moves by which a 'wandering minstrel' won the game and a night with the lady of the castle, as the tales suggested. So I wrote the chess match. If I'd been a medieval lady, and if a passing minstrel had played this game when I was lonely for a man, it would have won me over.

When I was seventeen and still a pupil, I ran the school chess club in Queen Anne Grammar School for Girls, York. I organised a match against the neighbouring boys' school: St Peter's. I was smug at beating their organiser, a boy my age, until he asked me out on a date. I realised he'd been distracted during the game and probably not played his best, so my win didn't really count, and I was very irritated. If only he'd read the poem I wrote ten years later, he could have used the game to better advantage – but I turned him down.

Young Love; Not Just Married; Leave in Silence

On TV, I watched an art historian's analysis of Watteau's *'Embarkation for Cythera,'* in which amorous couples are either heading for or leaving the *'Island of Love,'* and the painting inspired my own equally cynical triptych of stages in love.

i) Young love and accidental pregnancy.

ii) Marriage and adultery. Wedding cars often used to have *'Just Married'* signs on them, meaning *'Newly-Wed'* and I wanted the title to play on the idea that the marriage is stale, so that they are not 'just married' and that they are having affairs, so they are not 'just married' in that sense either.

iii) Divorce. The title comes from the Depeche Mode song and was a reaction to an American documentary in which divorcing couples aired all their grievances. I find that sordid and depressing. Nowadays, the detail would be on the social media and cell-phone pictures – even more sordid and depressing. I am a big fan of silence but – the fiction writer's paradox – the life shapes the writing. I am not, however, a golden retriever. Nor even a Great Pyrenees.

At this stage in my life, I didn't believe that any marriage was or could be happy. I was wrong.

If you liked my book, please help other readers find it by writing a review.

Thank you.

For exclusive offers and news of my books,
and a FREE ebook of
One Sixth of a Gill,
please visit jeangill.com and sign up for my newsletter.
This collection of shorts and poems was a finalist in
the Wishing Shelf and *SpaSpa Awards*.

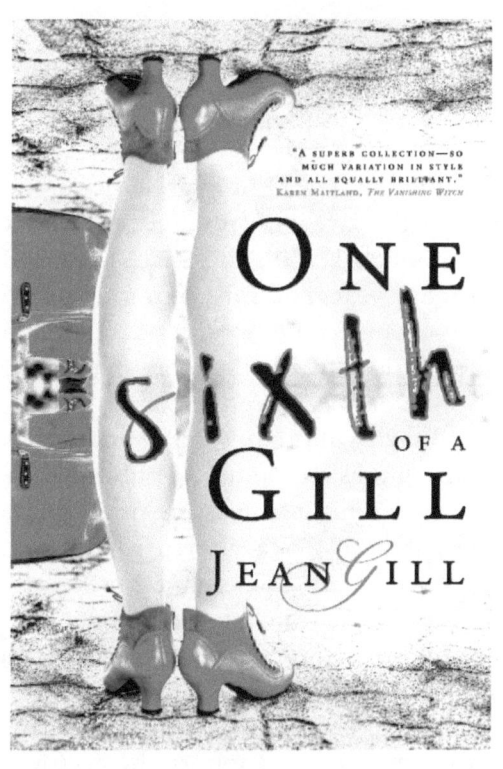

About the Author

I'm a Welsh writer and photographer living in the south of France with two scruffy dogs, a beehive named *Endeavour*, a Nikon D750 and a man. I taught English in Wales for many years and my claim to fame is that I was the first woman to be a secondary headteacher in Carmarthenshire. I'm mother or stepmother to five children so life has been pretty hectic.

I've published all kinds of books, both with conventional publishers and self-published. You'll find everything under my name from prize-winning poetry and novels, military history, translated books on dog training, to a cookery book on goat cheese. My work with top dog-trainer Michel Hasbrouck has taken me deep into the world of dogs with problems, and inspired one of my novels.

With Scottish parents, an English birthplace and French residence, I can support the winning team on most sporting occasions.

From Bedtime On

NEW edition with the true stories behind the poems.

The second collection of poetry from award-winning author Jean Gill retains the passion and spiky humour for which she is known but has matured into a unique, assured view of our world. Her most lyrical poems reveal a sensuality that lingers in the imagination.

'I would not give my eyes to tune pianos
but for one brightened night to read
the raised points of your skin with blind man's fingers
I might.'

Jean Gill's award-winning series
The Troubadours Quartet
History was never more exciting!

1150 in Provence

'Historical Fiction at its best.' Karen Charlton, *the Detective Lavender Mysteries*

Set in the period following the Second Crusade, Jean Gill's spellbinding romantic thrillers evoke medieval France with breathtaking accuracy. The characters leap off the page and include amazing women like Eleanor of Aquitaine and Ermengarda of Narbonne, who shaped history in battles and in bedchambers.

www.ingramcontent.com/pod-product-compliance
Lightning Source LLC
LaVergne TN
LVHW041224080526
838199LV00083B/3307